A Small Love Dictionary of
Untranslatable Japanese Words

Eleni Cay

A Small Love Dictionary of Untranslatable Japanese Words

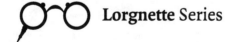 **Lorgnette** Series

First published in 2017
by Eyewear Publishing Ltd
Suite 333, 19-21 Crawford Street
Marylebone, London W1H 1PJ
United Kingdom

Typeset with graphic design by Edwin Smet
Author photograph by Jana Kussova
Printed in England by Lightning Source

ISBN 978-1-912477-34-0

Eyewear wishes to thank Jonathan Wonham for his generous patronage of our press.

WWW.EYEWEARPUBLISHING.COM

This book is dedicated to
all my present and future
Japanese friends.

Such is our way of thinking
– we find beauty not in the
thing itself but in the patterns
of shadows, the light and
the darkness, that one thing
against another creates.

– Junichiro Tanizaki, *In Praise of Shadows*

TABLE OF CONTENTS

AIKI (合気)

(n.): Blending/harmonising opposing forces within oneself

If I was the slaveholder of Time,
I would command it to selectively
numb the deeply entrenched,
and yet, elusive, memory of you.

I would make love colourless, remove
all signs and symbols that denote the
pulsing space between two people.

But, alas, until the glory of Time departs,
we will set, we will rise,
like a phoenix from the ashes
of its counterparts.

AMAE (甘え)

(v.): To behave in ways that implicitly request love or the indulgence of one's perceived needs

I roped my desires to your chest,
chained them into golden tokens of fidelity,
surrounding everything we touched.

I pledged my life to that chain, revered it like
an altar, offered pieces of myself every evening.

All that for the luminous ring of security, the promise
that when sudden frost kills the primroses,
my pain can liquidise into a little girl's tears.

AWARE (哀れ)

(n.): The bittersweetness of a brief, fading moment of transcendent beauty

Imagine that tonight the nightingale can sing
forever and the night is never done.

Black rays will curl up around our naked minds,
the glow worms will over-shine our past.

We will switch off the sun, make love timeless
and more than a few stars heaving in-between darkness.

DATSUZOKU (脱俗)

(n.): Freedom from habit, escape from the routine and conventional

Beneath a delicate lace
that can sustain morning tears
and summer fragrance,
your thin fingers walk my naked back,
tangling my hair into a chrysalis.

Love's membrane lures in more wishes,
unmercifully wraps them
before sucking out all their goodness.
Imprisoned in the sticky threads
we make love every night, nevertheless.

Until one morning, when the spider web
tears into two houses – with regret at one doorstep.

FUUBUTSUSHI (風物詩)

(n.): Stimuli or phenomena that evoke/remind one of a particular season

The clouds travel forth, indifferently.
Einstein ponders their movement,
Picasso their shapes,
they continue their never-ending movie.
The grasses release their tears,
ants bathe their wings.
Wild geese strike through,
colliding with Cupid's arrows,
fencing off the territory
set aside for broken lives.
A bullfinch passes under the damson trees,
the wind inhales in blue,
exhales in grey the human story.

GAMAN (我慢)

(n.): Patience, fortitude, endurance, self-control/restraint

Is it a white ribbon wrapped around my heart,
or a stray feather that drifts upwards?
Will it burn its barbules in the deep golden,
lose its words in the rosary prayer, or will it
bring me closer to the secret of divine mystery?

The sky folds the feather into its cupola,
blends it with billions of past prayers, wings of angels,
white doves. A cherub's little hands finger a tuba.
Desires grow, not in the borderlines, but from the middle end,
the rusty tones of Cohen's hallelujah.

GIRI (義理)

(n.): Duty, obligation, a debt of honour. It is defined as 'to serve one's superiors with a self-sacrificing devotion' by Namiko Abe

Against the theory of wingless flights,
the cherries in the Vancouver street dress in the same garment
as the sharp crystals that stifled them some days ago.

They become a cloud, let the white cotton fall down,
one by one, no matter the blackness around.

Against the myth of broken hearts, they make you grapple with
the seal who returns to the land to give birth to young
and then teaches them to swim.

Against any unexpected storm, they let the time change
the colour of their skin, with no recrimination.

GORAIKOU (御来光)

(n.): Lit. 'sacred delivery of light'; e.g., sunlight seen from the top of Mount Fuji

Wordless melodies unfold the vast space
where we came from but no longer belong.

We needed to hurt, we needed to go wrong
to have an offering for the Lord's mercy.

One day, stripped of our vivid tempers and
textured dresses, we will rise to the sublime.

Guided by His grace, unfinished memories
will rock all tones to silence, we will climb

the smooth bones of time,
begging for forgiveness.

IKIGAI (生き甲斐)

(n.): A 'reason for being'; the sense that it is worthwhile to continue living

Every night, I present my body in soft Egyptian cotton,
together with the wild tangos I no longer dance.

Assuming a defenceless posture, I lay open my soul,
let the Moon, for a whimsical while, take me to the stars.

In the morning, when all the magic is returned to the sky,
I put on a clean shirt to protect me from having to relive

the sacrifice. With no time to grieve,
I accept that dreams promise more than life can give.

KAWAAKARI (かわあかり)

(n.): Literally, 'river bright'; the glow/gleam of the river at dusk (or in the darkness)

A heartbreak dries on the blades of a wounded maiden grass.
Tonight, her innocent flowers will not swan the dark sky.
They will waft above the gathering tears, let the birds slice
them into orange segments to feed the greedy air.

The wind flutes the words you forgot to say when you left.
Tonight, I don't need your voice to fulfil my prayer.
The moon draws breath into unborn clouds, its bright light
stirs the one who incarnates distance and indifference.

KINTSUGI (金継ぎ)

(n.): Literally, 'golden joinery' (the art of repairing broken pottery using gold); metaphorically meaning to render our flaws and fault-lines beautiful and strong

Nectarine flowers fill the summer with desires.
The hunger craves rise, everywhere, anytime,
you cannot predict a specific colour of the sky.

You know you will get hurt by the bright beauty,
but you cannot make sense of what has befallen you.
Yearning to be emptied like snow into a dull country,

you release everything you ever possessed,
in deep hope of conquering grey with blue.

KOKO (枯高)

(n.): Weathered beauty, austere sublimity

The human child is born hungry.
Constantly on the hunt
for more.

Love turns to deep hurt
because of the moving lashes
in his soul.

Wrapped around the wind's neck,
wild grasses never leave
their home.

They stay loyal to the bulb,
to the soil.

KOKORO (心)

(n.): Heart and mind (and even spirit) combined

I pluck the harp on your chest.
Hair by hair, I play you songs upon request.

I travel through smooth valleys, rough terrain.
Cell by cell, I engrave your back chain.

Your lip responds,
casting our bodies
into eternal bonds.

In the melody
only you and I understand
we dance each other to No Man's Land.

KOI NO YOKAN (恋の予感)

(n.): The feeling on meeting someone that falling in love will be inevitable

Walking down the five possible paths to freedom,
your tongue ends in the centre of my palm.

We have always echoed each other,
andante, allegro, then the original tempo.

There has never been a sequence
in our story, no moment has been privileged.

Just a bricolage of our own selves
throwing new empty vessels on a wheel.

MOKUSATSU (黙殺)

(v.): To ignore or keep silent (e.g., when rejecting a bargaining offer)

The Sun shines on the asphalt pavement, but there are
no dolphins to jump out, just blackness to melt.

Autumn leaves fly together with plastic bags,
share with them the tiny space on trimmed magnolias.

The birds' love songs sound every day the same,
they don't care that last night Juan hit Rosie in her face again.

Who cares about love and happiness?
The Moon's face remains wrinkless.

MONO NO AWARE (物の哀れ)

(n.): The pathos of understanding the transience of the world and its beauty

Your broad shoulders shift beneath a worn-out denim jacket,
as if they were wild horses, with a heavenly yet earthy presence
for no one but you to command.

For the promise of an escape from time I lose myself in
your land, enchanted by the woodsy tones of your touch,
each so delicate and telling.

There has never been a beginning or end to our fairy tale,
we made it as we walked it, just like today
walks on yesterday.

NAKAMA (仲間)

(n.): Best friend, close buddy, one for whom one feels deep platonic love

I sip your words with a fine scotch whisky,
let them develop into a tropical storm.
You want to return to me like rain to river,
taste my wet body against yours,
make the same promise we did years ago.
Pressing on the thin skin of goodbyes
we spread the pain, as much as only lovers
who became best friends can.

OMOIYARI (おもいやり)

(n.): An intuitive understanding of others' desires, feelings and thoughts, and consequent action on the basis of this understanding

My desires saunter along the well-walked path towards you,
returning forlorn to the wretched knot at which hope roots.
I head-butt their calling, but they retrace their way,
pretend to sail upwind in a mauve-blue lightness
 – like a squirrel to the top of a pine.

I spin them, so fast that they become one bright circle,
dawning upon the four corners of Earth in the early hours.
In each corner, wise men ponder the genesis of sunflowers,
desperately trying to explain the origin of grey seeds
with dainty petals sewn around them.

SUNAO (素直)

(adj. n.): Meek, docile and submissive (in a positive, deferential way); authentic, and honest with oneself

His back curls itself within her breast, sketching
a near-perfect sphere, as if to reflect a deity on the ground.

For some years, that circle afforded them a structure
for a soft-bearing subjectivity, indicated a direction forward.

When it burst, there was no panic. No clarity.
Only an insipid feeling of lost homeland.

Just like when her cheeks got wetter,
even though they were cushioned in his hands.

SEIJAKU (静寂)

(n.): Literally, 'quiet' (sei) 'tranquillity' (jaku); silence, calm, serenity (especially in the midst of activity or chaos)

The dawn
surrenders to the sun,
personifying what we become
when we fuse into one.

A Maltese cat
folded in the windowsill
breathes heavily
like a new-born child.

SHIBUMI (渋味)

(n.): Simple, subtle, unobtrusive and effortless beauty

There was just a faint cry when the pearl was born.

The mermaids watched her in awe. *Leggiero*
she said goodbye to the sea.

Deep waters dried out her tears,
stonefish withdrew towards complete silence.

Her soft sheen will now spellbind the creatures
living on the islands.

UTURA-UTURA (うつらうつら)

(Gitaigo, v.): To drift between sleep and wakefulness

It's late night and the sound of the lyre
has almost vanished, but nothing
can rock Cupid to sleep.
He knows not if it is right
that the wind sometimes blows
the sparks into a fire and sometimes
into an inferno,
but he knows it would be worse
if he ever stopped. Morning glory will
ignite more stories on his bow, not
too different from the ones we lived before.

ACKNOWLEDGEMENTS

The English translations and the choice of words were taken from Dr Lomas' positive lexicography (an on-going research project into 'untranslatable' words undertaken at the University of East London).
They have been used with kind permission of Dr Lomas.

'Mono no aware (Timeless seduction)' was published in *South Poetry* Issue 55, April 2017. An earlier version of the poem 'Datsuzoku (脱俗)' was published by Westbury Arts Centre in *Autumn Dedications*.